GREATEST OF ALL TIME SPORTS STARS

THE GREATEST BASEBALL PLAYERS OF ALL TIME

BY MICHAEL RAJCZAK

Gareth Stevens PUBLISHING

Please visit our website, www.garethstevens.com. For a free color catalog of all our high-quality books, call toll free 1-800-542-2595 or fax 1-877-542-2596.

Cataloging-in-Publication Data

Names: Rajczak, Michael.
Title: The greatest baseball players of all time / Michael Rajczak.
Description: New York : Gareth Stevens Publishing, 2020. | Series: Greatest of all time: sports stars | Includes glossary and index.
Identifiers: ISBN 9781538247716 (pbk.) | ISBN 9781538247730 (library bound) | ISBN 9781538247723
(6 pack)
Subjects: LCSH: Baseball players–Rating of–United States–Juvenile literature. | Baseball players–United States–Statistics. | Baseball players–Biography–Juvenile literature. | Baseball–Records–United States–Juvenile literature. | Baseball–United States–History–Juvenile literature.
Classification: LCC GV865.A1 R33 2019 | DDC 796.3570922 B–dc23

First Edition

Published in 2020 by
Gareth Stevens Publishing
111 East 14th Street, Suite 349
New York, NY 10003

Designer: Katelyn E. Reynolds
Editor: Emily Mahoney

Photo credits: Cover, p. 1 Jayne Kamin-Oncea/Getty Images; cover, pp. 1–32 (series art) Dmitry Kostrov/Shutterstock.com; cover, pp. 1–32 (series background) rangizzz/Shutterstock.com; p. 4 Sporting News via Getty Images via Getty Images; p. 5 Hy Peskin/Getty Images; pp. 7, 22 (Ty Cobb) Mark Rucker/Transcendental Graphics, Getty Images; p. 8 Rick Stewart/Getty Images; p. 9 Otto Greule Jr/Getty Images; pp. 10, 23 (Roberto Clemente) Focus on Sport/Getty Images; pp. 11, 20, 25 Bettmann/Getty Images; p. 13 The Stanley Weston Archive/Getty Images; p. 14 Transcendental Graphics/Getty Images; p. 15 Photo File/MLB Photos via Getty Images; p. 16 Chris Hondros/Newsmakers/Getty Images; p. 17 Doug Pensinger/Getty Images; pp. 19, 21 Louis Requena/Stringer/Major League Baseball/Getty Images; p. 22 (Barry Bonds) Jed Jacobsohn/Getty Images; p. 22 (Mickey Mantle) MLB Photos via Getty Images; p. 23 (Ted Williams) Getty Images; p. 23 (Ken Griffey Jr.) Stephen Dunn/Getty Images; pp. 27–28 (baseball graphic) KoQ Creative/Shutterstock.com; p. 28 Ezra O. Shaw /Allsport/Getty Images; p. 29 Julio Aguilar/Getty Images.

Printed in the United States of America

CPSIA compliance information: Batch #CW20GS: For further information contact Gareth Stevens, New York, New York at 1-800-542-2595.

CONTENTS

WORDS IN THE GLOSSARY APPEAR IN **BOLD** TEXT THE FIRST TIME THEY ARE USED IN THE TEXT.

WHAT MAKES A PLAYER GREAT

Being considered one of the all-time great baseball players is quite an honor. Being great means you are one of the best at something. In baseball, that may mean hitting the most home runs or having a high batting average. A pitcher may be thought of as one of the greats if he has many strikeouts or a lot of wins.

Great players demonstrate a very high skill level year after year. They react more quickly and correctly to challenging situations. They can keep their focus and tune out **distractions**. Speed, strength, self-discipline, **self-confidence**, and better-than-average eyesight are also qualities great players usually have.

BRADY ANDERSON

PITCHER DICK ELLSWORTH OF THE CHICAGO CUBS WON 22 GAMES IN 1963. IF HE HAD BEEN ABLE TO STRING TOGETHER MORE SEASONS LIKE THAT ONE GREAT YEAR, HE COULD HAVE BEEN CONSIDERED ONE OF THE GREATS.

GREAT—FOR A SHORT TIME

BEING ONE OF THE ALL-TIME GREATS MEANS PUTTING UP AMAZING NUMBERS EVERY YEAR FOR A LONG TIME. SOME PLAYERS HAD AMAZING SEASONS OR AMAZING GAMES, BUT COULDN'T STAY GREAT FOR THEIR ENTIRE CAREERS. BRADY ANDERSON HIT 50 HOME RUNS IN 1996 FOR THE BALTIMORE ORIOLES, THOUGH THE REST OF HIS 15-YEAR CAREER WAS FAIRLY AVERAGE. MEANWHILE, NEW YORK YANKEES PITCHER DON LARSEN IS BEST KNOWN FOR A SINGLE GAME. HE THREW A PERFECT GAME IN THE 1956 WORLD SERIES—PERFECT FOR A SINGLE DAY ON BASEBALL'S BIGGEST STAGE.

PITCHERS

Christy Mathewson was one of the most **dominant** pitchers of the early years of modern baseball, playing mostly for the New York Giants. From 1900 to 1917, he won 30 or more games in a season four times, and led the National League in strikeouts five times. Known as a fearless player, he threw mostly strikes, daring batters to hit his pitches.

Another all-time great pitcher was Walter Johnson. He led the American League in strikeouts 12 times, and he holds the major league record for most **shutouts** at 110. Maybe the most impressive fact is that he played for 21 years, from 1907 to 1927—all with one team, the Washington Senators.

UNLIKE TODAY, WHEN PITCHERS GENERALLY DON'T PITCH THE WHOLE BASEBALL GAME, PITCHERS LIKE MATHEWSON, JOHNSON, AND YOUNG (SHOWN HERE) WOULD USUALLY PITCH ALL NINE INNINGS OF A GAME.

THE BEST PITCHER AWARD

YOU MIGHT THINK THAT THE YEARLY AWARD FOR THE BEST PITCHER WOULD HAVE BEEN NAMED FOR EITHER MATHEWSON OR JOHNSON. INSTEAD, IT WAS NAMED FOR ANOTHER PITCHER FROM THE EARLY DAYS OF BASEBALL, CY YOUNG. FROM 1890 TO 1911, CY YOUNG WON 511 GAMES, WHICH IS STILL THE MAJOR LEAGUE BASEBALL (MLB) RECORD.

ROGER CLEMENS

Another great pitcher, Roger Clemens, won the Cy Young Award seven times, more than any other pitcher in history. The 11-time All-Star and two-time World Series Champion holds the record for most strikeouts in a game (20) and has the third-most career strikeouts (4,672).

Randy Johnson was the most feared pitcher of the modern era of baseball. Known as "The Big Unit," his blazing fastball was the stuff of legend. He struck out at least 329 batters for five seasons in a row. A 10-time All-Star, he won five Cy Young Awards during his 22-year career.

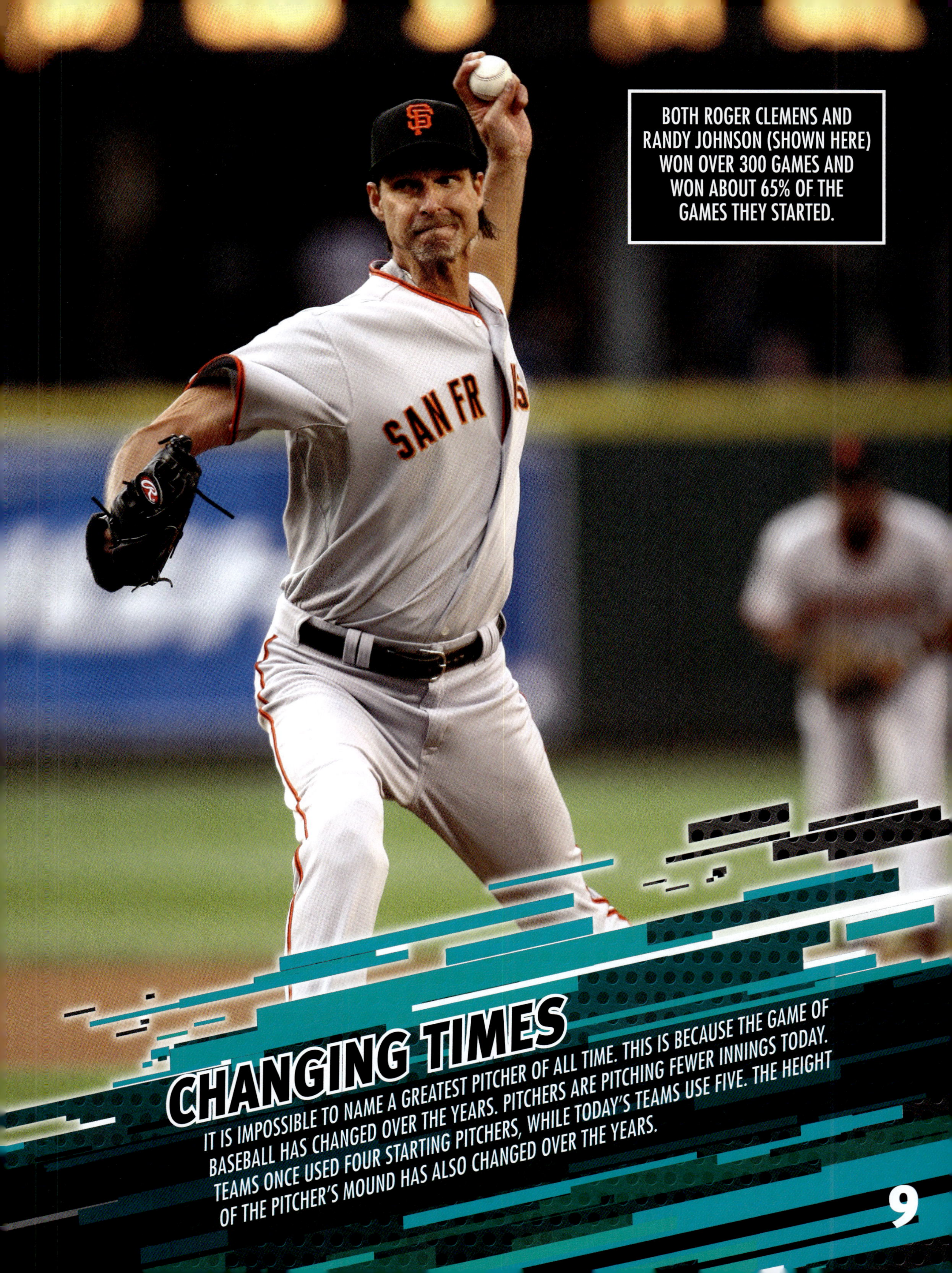

BOTH ROGER CLEMENS AND RANDY JOHNSON (SHOWN HERE) WON OVER 300 GAMES AND WON ABOUT 65% OF THE GAMES THEY STARTED.

CHANGING TIMES

IT IS IMPOSSIBLE TO NAME A GREATEST PITCHER OF ALL TIME. THIS IS BECAUSE THE GAME OF BASEBALL HAS CHANGED OVER THE YEARS. PITCHERS ARE PITCHING FEWER INNINGS TODAY. TEAMS ONCE USED FOUR STARTING PITCHERS, WHILE TODAY'S TEAMS USE FIVE. THE HEIGHT OF THE PITCHER'S MOUND HAS ALSO CHANGED OVER THE YEARS.

CATCHERS

Many consider Johnny Bench of the Cincinnati Reds the greatest catcher of all time. He was a great hitter, smacking 389 home runs during his career, one of the highest totals of any catcher in history. He was also one of the best defensive catchers of all time. Winner of the Rookie of the Year Award in 1968, Bench went on to be named league MVP twice and MVP of the 1976 World Series.

Bench had a cannon for an arm. He perfected the use of a **hinged** catcher's glove. This allowed him to catch one-handed and more quickly grasp the ball to throw out a runner trying to steal a base. Bench also won 10 Gold Glove Awards for great fielding by a catcher.

JOHNNY BENCH

GREAT CATCHERS LIKE BENCH AND BERRA (SHOWN HERE) ARE LIKE THE FIELD GENERALS OF THEIR TEAM. THEY DIRECT THE DEFENSE AND HELP PITCHERS DECIDE WHICH PITCHES TO THROW.

AN AMAZING YANKEE

CATCHER YOGI BERRA PLAYED IN 10 NEW YORK YANKEE WORLD CHAMPIONSHIPS. HE WAS AN ALL-STAR AN AMAZING 15 TIMES, AND LEAGUE MVP THREE TIMES. IT IS SAID THAT HE COULD HIT ANY PITCH. YOGI WAS KNOWN FOR HIS SENSE OF HUMOR AND FUNNY SAYINGS, SUCH AS "IT AIN'T OVER TILL IT'S OVER."

FIRST BASEMEN

Lou Gehrig remains possibly the most respected man ever to play baseball. Not only did he play in 2,130 games in a raw, he is among the best hitters and run producers in history. Gehrig scored over 100 runs and batted in at least 100 more runs for 13 straight years.

A **humble** man, especially compared to his very outgoing teammate Babe Ruth, Gehrig was a seven-time All-Star and six-time World Series Champion with the New York Yankees. His career and life were cut short due to a terrible disease, called amyotrophic lateral sclerosis (ALS). It causes a person's muscles to gradually weaken over time. The illness is now known as Lou Gehrig's Disease.

AT AGE 36, LOU GEHRIG WAS THE YOUNGEST PLAYER EVER ELECTED TO THE BASEBALL HALL OF FAME.

STAN THE MAN

A THREE-TIME MVP, STAN MUSIAL WAS ALSO NAMED AN ALL-STAR 24 TIMES. LIKE MANY PLAYERS, MUSIAL PLAYED A CONSIDERABLE TIME IN THE OUTFIELD AS WELL AS FIRST BASE. MUSIAL WAS A .331 LIFETIME HITTER AND PLAYED ON THREE CHAMPIONSHIP TEAMS. STAN WAS NOT FLASHY, JUST A DEPENDABLE AND EXCELLENT PLAYER YEAR IN AND YEAR OUT.

SECOND BASEMEN

The **standard** of excellence at second base was set in the early days of baseball. Rogers Hornsby was the greatest right-handed hitter of all time with a lifetime batting average of .358. Hornsby won seven batting titles. He was a player and manager who led the 1926 St. Louis Cardinals to the World Series Championship.

Hornsby had followed a simple rule about hitting: "Never get the idea that you can't hit a certain pitcher." He was known for his speed and hustle on the bases. Hornsby had 30 inside-the-park home runs and was known to stretch singles into doubles and even triples.

TO CELEBRATE THE ANNIVERSARY OF JACKIE ROBINSON BREAKING THE COLOR BARRIER, MLB RETIRED HIS NUMBER, 42. THIS MEANS THAT NOBODY ELSE CAN CHOOSE TO WEAR THIS NUMBER ON THEIR JERSEY.

NUMBER 42

JACKIE ROBINSON WAS THE ROOKIE OF THE YEAR AT AGE 28. HE IS KNOWN FOR BEING THE FIRST AFRICAN AMERICAN TO PLAY IN THE MAJOR LEAGUES. HE HANDLED ABUSE FROM FANS, AND EVEN PLAYERS, WITH DIGNITY. AS A PLAYER, HE WAS A SIX-TIME ALL-STAR AND WON THE MVP AWARD IN 1949.

SHORTSTOPS

Considered one of the greatest players of his era (1897-1917), Honus Wagner played for 21 seasons. He led the National League in batting average eight times, hitting at least .300 for 15 years. He was also known for being very strong and fast.

Wagner was an amazing shortstop. It was said that the only way to get a ball by him was to hit it 8 feet (2.4 m) over his head. He was known for turning double plays and ranking near the top of all fielding statistics year in and year out. Wagner was also recognized for his kindness and **sportsmanship** to teammates, fans, and even umpires.

HONUS WAGNER'S TRADING CARD WAS CREATED WITHOUT HIS PERMISSION BY A TOBACCO COMPANY. WHEN HE FOUND OUT, HE TOOK LEGAL ACTION TO STOP IT. HE DID NOT WANT HIS YOUNG FANS TO HAVE TO BUY CIGARETTES TO GET HIS CARD.

OMAR VIZQUEL IS SHOWN HERE COMPLETING HIS RECORD-BREAKING 1,591 DOUBLE PLAY TURNED BY A SHORTSTOP. HE BROKE THIS RECORD ON MAY 13, 2007.

A GREAT DEFENSIVE PLAYER

THE BEST FIELDING SHORTSTOP OF THE MODERN ERA WAS OMAR VIZQUEL. HIS 10 GOLD GLOVES AND LIFETIME FIELDING **PERCENTAGE** OF .9847 RANK HIM AS ONE OF THE BEST DEFENSIVE PLAYERS OF ALL TIME. VIZQUEL IS OFTEN OVERLOOKED IN FAVOR OF THE POWERFUL AND FLASHY YANKEE ALEX RODRIGUEZ, WHO PLAYED DURING THE SAME PERIOD OF TIME AND RANKS FOURTH IN CAREER HOME RUNS WITH 696.

THIRD BASEMEN

Philadelphia Phillies third baseman Mike Schmidt is nearly every expert's choice as the greatest third baseman of all time. His was an outstanding defensive fielder, winning the Gold Glove 10 times. He was also a great hitter. He tied Babe Ruth for the number of times he lead the league in home runs at eight. Schmidt was a three-time MVP and a 12-time All-Star.

Mike Schmidt led the Phillies to a World Series victory in 1980. In 1983, Schmidt won the Lou Gehrig Memorial Award for outstanding personal character and **integrity** both on and off the field. He is referred to as the greatest Phillies player of all time.

MIKE SCHMIDT WAS THE 1980 WORLD SERIES MVP AFTER HITTING TWO HOME RUNS AND HAVING SEVEN RUNS BATTED IN.

THE HOT CORNER

A THIRD BASEMAN HAS TO REACT AND THINK QUICKLY. PLAYING BASEBALL'S "HOT CORNER" OF THE INFIELD, A THIRD BASEMAN MUST BE ABLE TO MAKE THE LONG THROW TO FIRST. BALTIMORE ORIOLE BROOKS ROBINSON IS CONSIDERED BY MOST TO BE THE BEST-EVER DEFENSIVE THIRD BASEMAN. HE WON THE GOLD GLOVE AWARD AN INCREDIBLE 16 TIMES IN HIS 23-YEAR CAREER.

OUTFIELDERS

Hank Aaron was the first to break Babe Ruth's all-time home run record and he finished his 23-year career with a total of 755. That's an average of 37 homers a year! His 2,297 runs batted in remains the all-time record. He played in 25 All-Star games, the most of any player in the history of baseball.

Aaron won three Gold Gloves playing right field. He won the MVP Award in 1957, the year he led his Milwaukee Braves to the World Series Championship (the team later moved to Atlanta). After his baseball career, he began the "Hank Aaron Chasing the Dream Foundation" to help children in need reach their dreams.

HANK AARON CELEBRATES BREAKING BABE RUTH'S HOME RUN RECORD IN HIS HOME STADIUM IN ATLANTA.

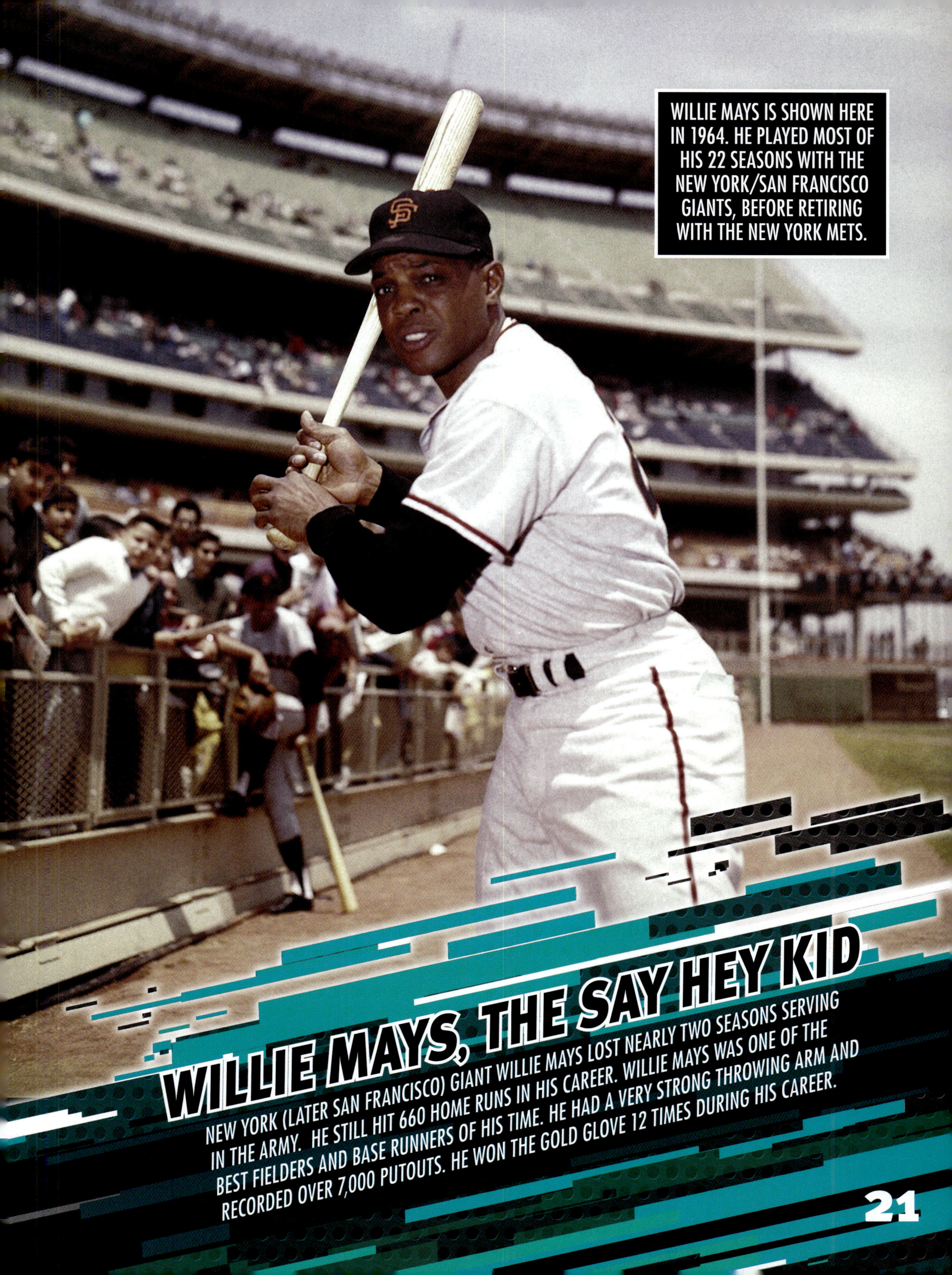

WILLIE MAYS IS SHOWN HERE IN 1964. HE PLAYED MOST OF HIS 22 SEASONS WITH THE NEW YORK/SAN FRANCISCO GIANTS, BEFORE RETIRING WITH THE NEW YORK METS.

WILLIE MAYS, THE SAY HEY KID

NEW YORK (LATER SAN FRANCISCO) GIANT WILLIE MAYS LOST NEARLY TWO SEASONS SERVING IN THE ARMY. HE STILL HIT 660 HOME RUNS IN HIS CAREER. WILLIE MAYS WAS ONE OF THE BEST FIELDERS AND BASE RUNNERS OF HIS TIME. HE HAD A VERY STRONG THROWING ARM AND RECORDED OVER 7,000 PUTOUTS. HE WON THE GOLD GLOVE 12 TIMES DURING HIS CAREER.

BARRY BONDS

BARRY BONDS HOLDS THE MAJOR LEAGUE RECORD FOR MOST HOME RUNS DURING A CAREER AT 762 AND THE SINGLE-SEASON RECORD OF 73, WHICH HE HIT IN 2001. HE WON MVP SEVEN TIMES AND THE GOLD GLOVE EIGHT TIMES. HIS POSSIBLE USE OF ILLEGAL **STEROIDS** HAS SO FAR KEPT HIM OUT OF THE HALL OF FAME.

TY COBB

TY COBB WAS ONE OF THE GREATEST HITTERS OF ALL TIME, WITH A LIFETIME BATTING AVERAGE OF .366. THIS IS STILL THE HIGHEST IN THE HISTORY OF BASEBALL. HE COLLECTED MORE THAN 4,000 HITS FOR HIS CAREER, ONE OF ONLY TWO PLAYERS TO TOP THAT MARK. HE WAS ALSO ONE OF THE BEST BASE STEALERS OF HIS ERA. KNOWN AS A FIERCE COMPETITOR WHO COULD SOMETIMES TURN VIOLENT ON THE FIELD, COBB WAS STILL ONE OF THE FIVE ORIGINAL PLAYERS CHOSEN FOR THE HALL OF FAME.

MICKEY MANTLE

MICKEY MANTLE HIT 536 HOME RUNS DURING THE 18 YEARS HE PLAYED WITH THE NEW YORK YANKEES, DESPITE STRUGGLING THROUGH MANY INJURIES. HE WAS THE BEST SWITCH-HITTER THE GAME HAS KNOWN, ABLE TO BAT FROM BOTH THE LEFT AND RIGHT SIDE OF THE PLATE.

TED WILLIAMS

TED WILLIAMS IS ONE OF THE BEST HITTERS OF ALL TIME. HE HIT 521 HOME RUNS AND LEADS ALL PLAYERS WITH A LIFETIME ON-BASE PERCENTAGE OF .482. THIS MEANS THAT OVER 48% OF THE TIME HE WAS AT BAT, HE WAS ABLE TO REACH BASE SAFELY, EITHER WITH A HIT, A WALK, OR BEING HIT BY A PITCH. HE ACHIEVED GREATNESS EVEN THOUGH HE MISSED FIVE SEASONS DUE TO MILITARY SERVICE.

KEN GRIFFEY JR.

KEN GRIFFEY JR. PLAYED FOR 22 SEASONS AND HIT 630 HOME RUNS. HE WON 10 GOLD GLOVE AWARDS AND WAS AN ALL-STAR 13 TIMES. HIS BEST SEASON WAS 1997, WHEN HE WAS NAMED MVP AND HIT 56 HOME RUNS.

ROBERTO CLEMENTE

ROBERTO CLEMENTE WAS ONE OF THE BEST DEFENDING OUTFIELDERS OF ALL TIME, TIED WITH WILLIE MAYS FOR THE MOST GOLD GLOVES AS AN OUTFIELDER. CONSIDERED THE FIRST GREAT HISPANIC PLAYER, HE LED HIS PITTSBURG PIRATES TO TWO WORLD SERIES CHAMPIONSHIPS. HE WAS KILLED IN A PLANE CRASH FLYING FOOD AND MEDICINE TO EARTHQUAKE SURVIVORS IN 1972.

BABE RUTH

Babe Ruth has been often called the greatest player of all time. He was certainly the most popular figure in baseball during his era, thanks largely to his ability to hit home runs. Over his 22-year career, Babe hit 714 home runs, including 60 in 1927 alone! For many years, both of these records were considered unbreakable.

Because Babe Ruth hit so many home runs, baseball became more exciting and popular. Before him, even great hitters mostly hit singles, doubles, and triples. Other players copied Babe's style. The Yankees went from being a losing team to the most popular team in American sports. Ruth's Yankees won four World Series Championships. He was one of the five original members of the Baseball Hall of Fame.

AFTER LEADING BOSTON TO THREE WORLD SERIES CHAMPIONSHIPS, GEORGE HERMAN "BABE" RUTH WAS SOLD TO THE NEW YORK YANKEES FOR $125,000.

THE BABE STARTED IN BOSTON

THOUGH HE IS KNOWN MOSTLY FOR HIS TIME AS A HOME-RUN HITTER FOR THE YANKEES, BABE WAS ONCE A TERRIFIC STARTING PITCHER FOR THE BOSTON RED SOX. HE PROVED TO BE TOO GOOD OF A HITTER TO JUST PLAY AS A PITCHER ONCE A WEEK. BOSTON BEGAN PLAYING HIM IN THE OUTFIELD. RUTH, WHOSE REAL FIRST NAME WAS GEORGE, PLAYED SIX SEASONS WITH THE BOSTON RED SOX, WINNING 89 GAMES PITCHING.

MORE GREATS

ROGER MARIS

ROGER MARIS WAS THE UNLIKELY SLUGGER TO BREAK BABE RUTH'S RECORD OF 60 HOME RUNS IN A SEASON. HE WAS A SIMPLE MAN, HUMBLE AND POLITE, A BIG DIFFERENCE FROM THE FLASHY BABE. IN FACT, RUTH WAS SO BELOVED BY YANKEES FANS, SOME PEOPLE DIDN'T LIKE IT WHEN MARIS HIT 61 HOME RUNS IN 1961—EVEN THOUGH MARIS WAS A YANKEE, TOO!

MARIANO RIVERA

NEW YORK YANKEE MARIANO RIVERA HOLDS THE RECORD FOR THE MOST SAVES BY A PITCHER AT 652. HIS 2019 SELECTION TO BASEBALL'S HALL OF FAME IS THE ONLY TIME A PLAYER RECEIVED 100% OF ALL POSSIBLE VOTES.

RICKY HENDERSON

RICKY HENDERSON IS THE ONLY PLAYER TO STEAL OVER 1,000 BASES. HIS 1,406 STOLEN BASES IS A RECORD THAT MAY NEVER BE BROKEN.

NOLAN RYAN

NOLAN RYAN PITCHED SEVEN NO-HITTERS, THREE MORE THAN ANYONE ELSE. HE ALSO HOLDS THE RECORD FOR MOST CAREER STRIKEOUTS (5,714) AND FOR THE FASTEST PITCH OF ALL TIME, THROWING THE BALL 108.5 MPH (174.6 KM/H).

GREG MADDUX

GREG MADDUX WAS A DIFFERENT TYPE OF PITCHER. NOLAN RYAN, ROGER CLEMENS, AND RANDY JOHNSON WERE HARD-THROWING STRIKEOUT ARTISTS. MADDUX GOT PEOPLE OUT USING EXCELLENT CONTROL, THROWING THE BALL RIGHT WHERE HE WANTED. HE LED THE LEAGUE IN ERA FOUR TIMES AND WON 355 GAMES DURING HIS CAREER.

BILL MAZEROSKI

BILL MAZEROSKI OF THE PITTSBURGH PIRATES HIT ONE OF THE GREATEST HOME RUNS OF ALL TIME IN THE 1960 WORLD SERIES. THE DECIDING GAME SEVEN WAS AGAINST THE MIGHTY NEW YORK YANKEES. WITH THE SCORE TIED IN THE BOTTOM OF THE NINTH INNING, MAZEROSKI SMACKED A HOMER THAT **INSTANTLY** WON THE WORLD SERIES FOR THE PIRATES.

TRIS SPEAKER

TRIS SPEAKER BEGAN HIS 22-YEAR CAREER IN 1907. HE STILL HOLDS THE MAJOR LEAGUE RECORD FOR HITTING 792 DOUBLES. TRIS ADDED AN **IMPRESSIVE** 222 TRIPLES. HIS .345 LIFETIME BATTING AVERAGE IS ONE OF THE BEST OF ALL TIME.

JOE DIMAGGIO

JOE DIMAGGIO PLAYED FOR 13 SEASONS AND WAS AN ALL-STAR EVERY YEAR. HE WAS NAMED AMERICAN LEAGUE MVP THREE TIMES. JOE SERVED THREE YEARS OF MILITARY SERVICE IN THE MIDDLE OF HIS CAREER. HE ALSO SET A RECORD BY HITTING IN 56 CONSECUTIVE GAMES.

BASEBALL HALL OF FAME

The Baseball Hall of Fame and Museum is located in the quiet town of Cooperstown, New York. Although various forms of a baseball-like game had been played for years, a popular local myth claimed that Abner Doubleday created baseball in 1839. The story stuck long enough for local businessman Stephen Clark to get permission to create the Hall of Fame in Cooperstown.

Being chosen to be in the Baseball Hall of Fame is the highest honor in baseball. It means you are the very best of the best. What these players achieved will always be considered great because they have been **inducted** into the Hall of Fame.

MORE THAN 19,000 PEOPLE HAVE PLAYED MAJOR LEAGUE BASEBALL DURING ITS LONG HISTORY. THERE ARE JUST 232 PLAYERS IN THE HALL OF FAME. THE HALL OF FAME MUSEUM FEATURES JERSEYS, BATS, BALLS, AND OTHER HISTORIC BASEBALL ITEMS.

MIKE TROUT IS A CENTER FIELDER WHO PLAYS FOR THE LOS ANGELES ANGELS. HE IS AN EIGHT-TIME ALL-STAR, AND HE WON THE AMERICAN LEAGUE MVP AWARD IN BOTH 2014 AND 2016. TROUT IS CONSIDERED ONE OF THE BEST ALL-AROUND PLAYERS IN THE HISTORY OF BASEBALL. AND HE'S STILL GOING! IF HE KEEPS IT UP, TROUT IS ON TRACK TO BECOME ONE OF THE GREATEST PLAYERS OF ALL TIME.

GETTING INTO THE HALL

IT ISN'T EASY GETTING INTO THE HALL OF FAME. FIRST, A PLAYER MUST MEET CERTAIN RULES SET UP BY THE HALL. THEY NEED TO HAVE PLAYED IN THE MAJOR LEAGUES FOR AT LEAST 10 YEARS AND BE RETIRED FOR FIVE SEASONS BEFORE THEY HAVE A CHANCE. THEN, IT'S UP TO BASEBALL WRITERS. MEMBERS OF THE BASEBALL WRITERS ASSOCIATION OF AMERICA VOTE ON WHO IS CHOSEN FOR INDUCTION IN COOPERSTOWN.

GLOSSARY

distraction: something that causes you to lose focus on a goal

dominant: the most powerful or strongest

hinged: describing where two things connect that allows them to open and close like a door

humble: not boastful; simple; modest

impressive: having a lasting effect; something of very high quality

induct: to vote into membership

instantly: right away

integrity: honesty

percentage: part of 100. For example 48 out of 100 is 48 percent.

self-confidence: believing you have the skills needed to do something

shutout: when the other team is not able to score a point

sportsmanship: a way of behaving in sports that includes respecting rules, others, and the outcome of a game

standard: a guide, example, or model

steroids: substances used by some athletes to increase muscle size or strength. Their use is not legal in most professional sports.